EAMES

© 2004 Assouline Publishing
601 West 26th Street, 18th Floor
New York, NY 10001, USA
Tel.: 212-989-6769 Fax: 212-647-0005

www.assouline.com

First published by Éditions Assouline, Paris

Translated from the French by Uniontrad

Color separation: GECM (France)

Printed in China ✿

ISBN: 9782843234200

10 9 8 7 6 5 4

EAMES

Furniture 1941-1978

BRIGITTE FITOUSSI

ASSOULINE

An American Myth

"Eames furniture are the key products of a bygone era.
They continue to convey the vitality and optimism
of the era in which they were designed:
an era when anything seemed possible,
when you could still idealize furniture.
That's why they have become mythical[1]."

ROLF FEHLBAUM

Pioneers of the 1950s and of the optimistic *American way of life*, designers Charles and Ray Eames created the greatest modern furniture "classics" between 1941 and 1978. They became masters in the art of armchair design, making it their specialty, and they offered a unique combination of technology, organic forms and new materials. The *Plywood Chairs LCW* and *DCW* (1946), the *Lounge Chair* (1956) and the *Aluminum Group* (1958) have become true symbols of design and remain references that are still produced today. As in art, they are emblematic objects, representing much more than just an armchair: the idea was to create a new consumer

4

product with high aesthetic value, without making compromises. The Eameses showed that through technology – for example, by assembling contrasting materials – it was possible to make beautiful objects. It was their drive to experiment, their vibrant "let's do it" philosophy that still makes us dream. Inheriting this spirit and carrying it on is perhaps a way to reveal the beauty of that alliance between art, nature and industry.

The Heritage

In a period such as ours, where objects are caught up in the runaway spiral of novelty, endlessly and seamlessly replacing each other without surprises, the Eameses' creations take us back to hap- pier times. Times when belief in strong ideas generated true ideals. Most of the current creators, architects and designers, no matter how famous or different they are – from Norman Foster to Jean Nouvel, from Vico Magistretti to Antonio Citterio, from Philippe Starck to Alberto Meda, and from Christophe Pillet to Jasper Morrison – are unanimously inspired by the Eameses' work. Beyond their differences, in their approach to design, all these creators have inherited the Eames spirit – perhaps this is a telltale sign of their genius. They are all fed up with products made only to be incorporated among existing products: another sofa, another chair, etc. Like the Eameses in their time, they would like to design necessary objects.

It is a flaw of current design that novelty must be justified, while the idea of contemporaneity is getting harder and harder to define. Everyone is looking for a level of "gratuitousness" in the act of creation, one not dictated by the laws of marketing, which are often off the mark. The word "design" no longer suggests that idea of purity and progress it conveyed originally, and with which the Eameses identified. In their day, it was a magic word.

That is why the wholehearted dedication of Charles and Ray Eames to creating beautiful and top-quality mass-market products, and the joy imparted through their free forms, gave rise to the myth of a human and sensual modernity. That is also why new generations of designers currently look for guidance from America of the 1950s. "You have to do the things you believe in, and drop all the others[2]," said Charles Eames, guided by his faith in social and humanistic progress. He embraced the world of design the way others take a religious vow.

Charles's Roots

At the age of 52, Charles's father, Charles Ormand Eames, married Céline Lambert, a very pretty woman who was much younger than him. She came from a good catholic family of French origin (her father was Alsatian), while he came from a family of English Methodists. Charles Eames was born in 1907 in Saint Louis, Missouri. Mr. Eames senior raised his son in the protestant tradi-tion, instilling in him a sense of duty, conscientiousness and courage at a very young age. His education was strict, yet not completely puritanical. Charles Eames remembers a peaceful childhood in a "wonderful and respectable middle-class family[3]." His father was a security officer for Pinkerton at the St. Louis train station, but his hobbies were painting and photography. It was probably by practicing these arts as an amateur that he sparked young Eames's creative energy. But the relationship between father and son was fairly distant, given his father's advanced years. Charles was especially close to his mother. He was only 12 when his father died in 1919. He inherited his father's passion for photography – and his old cameras (until then, he had never been allowed to touch them). This passion later transformed into a complete fascination for all the visual arts. With his father gone, Charles was quickly saddled with responsibilities. As the only man in his family, he grew up surrounded by his mother, his sister Adèle and two aunts who came to live with them. At the age of 14, when he entered Yeatman High School in the north of St. Louis, he also worked at the Laclede steel company near Venice, Illinois – part-time after school, and full-time in the summer. He exhibited such impressive drawing skills that he was quickly promoted to industrial draftsman in the design department. Through this job, and his skills in mathematics and science, the idea of becoming an architect gradually emerged.

In 1925, he was admitted to Washington University in St. Louis to study architecture. He immediately developed a dislike for academics and the close-mindedness in this university. He was especially enthusiastic about the architect Frank Lloyd Wright, who was criticized at that time by most of his professors. Despite young Eames's singular ways, he won two honor prizes for the "ultramodernity" of his projects. But he quickly left the university in 1928, and two years later he founded his own office in St. Louis: Gray and Eames. His associate was Charles M. Gray, whom he met at the Trueblood and Graf architectural office where he "drudged" summers when he was in college. In the meantime, in 1929, he married Catherine Dewey Woerman, a student at Washington University. For their honeymoon, they took a trip to Europe (a gift from his father-in-law), following in the footsteps of the great modern architects. He enthusiastically discovered the buildings made by Mies van der Rohe, Walter Gropius, Le Corbusier and Henry van de Velde.

Cranbrook Academy of Art

When one of his projects was published in an architecture magazine, Charles Eames was contacted in 1938 by Finnish architect Eliel Saarinen. The director of the Cranbrook Academy of Art near Detroit, Saarinen invited Eames to take architecture and design classes. He was 31 years old. Two years later, he became head of the industrial design department, working part-time at the Saarinen office. At Cranbrook, new perspectives were opening up for young American architects: The influence of Scandinavian forms, especially the work of Alvar Aalto, combined with the new interest in the ideas of the Arts and Crafts movement, offered an alternative to the modern international style. The eternal 20th-century dream of combining art and industry hovered over this unconventional school where students were constantly encouraged to engage in all-out experimentation with forms, materials and techniques.

In the 1930s and '40s, Cranbrook was the breeding ground for some of the greatest designers of this century, including of course Charles Eames. Eames had contact with such people as Florence Knoll, Tony Rosenthal, Don Albinson, Harry Bertoia, and Saarinen's son, Eero, who became his associate in his new experiments with furniture. This encounter was decisive. In 1940, Charles and Eero participated in a competition organized by the New York Museum of Modern Art (MoMA), *Organic Design in Home Furnishing*, and won first prize. The judges included such figures as Alvar Aalto and Marcel Breuer, names that made the young duo dream. As did *Bloomingdale's*, one of the sponsors of the competition, that was to sell the winning furniture in their department store (unfortunately, with the advent of the war, this wonderful opportunity never was realized). The prizewinning project consisted of a series of chairs, tables and storage units in molded plywood, an inexpensive wood they fashioned by developing a new manufacturing process intended for mass-production. The furniture was built by alternating layers of wooden slats and glue. Four to six hours before assembly, the layers were subjected to pressure and heat in a mold to obtain the desired three-dimensional, curved shape. The furniture adventure had begun...even though these first attempts at formed, molded plywood never got beyond the prototype stage – Charles and Eero did not succeed in mass-producing them.

Charles Meets Ray

In 1940, at Cranbrook, Charles was married and father to a little girl, Lucia, aged 10, when he met Bernice Alexandra Kaiser (nicknamed Ray), born in 1912 in Sacramento, California.

Ray was 28 years old and still a student. She was an artist and a member of American Abstract Artists, a group with a strong focus on contemporary art. She had also studied in New York with the German painter Hans Hofmann. Arp, Miró, Picasso and Kandinsky were her first influences and they kindled her interest in organic forms.

After her mother's death in 1940, Ray was encouraged by Benjamin Baldwin, another of Hofmann's students, to study at the Cranbrook Academy of Art. As her older sister died when Ray was only a few months old, her parents were always overprotective. She had a hard time cutting the family umbilical cord. Thus, it was relatively late in her life that she decided to develop her passion for new art forms.

At Cranbrook, she participated in the *Organic Design in Home Furnishing* competition, helping with the sketches and models of Don Albinson and Harry Bertoia. Her encounter with Charles Eames that year was like a bolt of lightning. It was love at first sight, followed by their wedding in the next year: Charles married Ray in 1941, in Chicago. The celebration took place at a friend's house. They then left for Los Angeles, California, and began their famed career.

Their oceanfront home in Pacific Palisades near Santa Monica was part of the ambitious *Case Study Houses* program launched in 1945 by John Entenza, director of the Californian magazine *Art & Architecture*, which partly sponsored the project. The theme was prefabrication, mass production and the industrialization of residential buildings. Each Southern California house had to be a prototype of modern lifestyle and conducive to improving the daily life of lower middle-class families. The program was implemented between 1945 and 1966, but of the 36 models proposed, only 23 were actually built.

These *Case Study Houses* were indicative of the idyllic vision of progress that was pervasive at the time. The houses were meant to provide answers to the problems faced by architects, contractors and potential customers, all of whom were trying to deal with the financial hardships and inflation of the postwar period.

The requirements were a flat roof deck, a modular design and a (preferably steel) frame. The resulting series of houses was of exceptional architectural quality and daring that fit perfectly into the natural environment. The houses of Richard Neutra, Pierre Koening, Edward Killingsworth and Raphaël Soriano can still be admired on the West Coast. So is the Eames house. High-tech statements, both *Case Study House no.* 8 and John Entenza's house were designed by Charles Eames and Eero Saarinen. It was their only architectural collaboration. Designed in 1945 and called the *Bridge House*, it was not built until 1949, after the plans had been completely reworked by Charles and Ray, who realized that the initial project did not take into sufficient account the magnificent site upon which they would build. In the end, the house, which included a living space and working space, was an elegant illustration of the couple's philosophy: a non-dogmatic example of modernity, filtered by the Californian sun. "Maximum volume, minimum materials[4]." They lived out their entire lives in this house.

Husband and Wife: a Collective Work

The spirit of an engineer and the precision of an architect combined with the soul and eye of an artist. The alliance of two different experiences: such is the foundation of the Eameses' collective work. Yet people often noticed only Charles. It is true that, given his extreme perfectionism, he made all the decisions. No matter what the project, and regardless of the skills of his numerous collaborators, not a single detail escaped him. His education had made him extremely strict, and his capacity for work was unlimited. Demanding of himself, so he was of those close to him. Working for the Eameses was a tremendous source of enthusiasm, but the master's discipline was often difficult for his employees to bear. In the office no music, chatting or chewing gum was allowed. "The projects were exciting, but working at the Eames Office was considered to be 'like gentle agony'," one reads in the biography written by John and Marilyn Neuhart, two of their most faithful collaborators.

Until 1978, all Ray's works, except for several drawings for the cover of *Art & Architecture* in the early 1940s, were done in association with her husband. In fact, Ray only began to value her work after she met the man she was to marry. From painting she shifted to other means of expression, devoting herself to the projects she shared with Charles. "I never stopped painting," she claimed, "I simply changed my palette."

Like any abstract artist, Ray had an eye for shape, color and composition. She chose all the fabrics and coverings. She was often the origin of the "Eames look," but her perception of design always had to pass through the filter of her husband's and the office's philoso-phy. She would suffer when her technical deficiencies would force her out of the main picture.

Charles the architect – he preferred that appellation to "designer" – approached design from the standpoints of structure, technology and problem-solving.

They were equal in their quest for precision and perfection, and always pushed a project to its outer limits. One thing is undeniable: all of their work, whether their house, their furniture or their toys, films and exhibitions, was the product of a true fusion of their sensitivities. Together they were fascinated by organic forms and new materials, the bridges between art and industry. Their approach was inspired by modern sculpture as much as by "mechanical construction, which uses materials according to their structural qualities[5]." Their collaboration made them the "most creative and most productive designer couple of the 20th century[6]."

Design for Everyone

Their work remains one of the main influences in the history of design – especially as time progresses and lack of direction leads designers to seek out their roots. This is probably because their work has always been accessible to a large audience. The Eameses were neither elitist nor dogmatic, and they succeeded in making general consumer products of such "aesthetic class" that they have become mythical.

Yet these products were designed without compromise, never betraying their aspirations and desires, and never dictated by marketing factors.

Charles hated the idea of style as much as he hated the idea of "doing something new."

However, he liked the idea that a product could mellow with age, and he designed a wide range of variations for each given model.

While not minimalistic, Eames furniture expresses the ideal of reduction and transparency. Nothing was to be superfluous; nothing was made if it was not needed. To the Eameses, technology was not an end in itself, it was guided by philosophy rather than aesthetics, by industry rather than craftsmanship. It was a source of boundless experimentation.

The couple wanted to make affordable, comfortable industrial products for everyone. "The most, the best, for the most people, using the smallest amount of money[7]."

Some of their fiberglass and plastic chairs, like the *Stacking Chair* or the famous *Wire Chair*, made of steel wire, sold by the millions.

In 1974, *Fortune Magazine* estimated that the Eameses received $15,000 every month in royalties for the sale of their furniture alone. But whatever they earned was usually spent on research and development for projects that exceeded their budgets.

The couple did not appear to be interested in money and continued to live a very simple life. While they were symbols of a booming consumer society, they did not partake.

The Art of Sitting

The primary effort of the Eameses' work on furniture focused on the armchair. Between 1941 and 1978, they designed more than 20 models, mostly unique pieces, and developed know-how in the "art of sitting." Materials, structure and comfort were the key words.

Their chairs used the expressive potential of new modern materials – plywood, plastic, aluminum and fiberglass – while adapting them to the fundamental needs of the human body. The Eameses sought beauty in technology, combined with what knowledge they could glean from nature. In this respect, the influence of the Finnish architect Alvar Aalto was essential to their work. They were fascinated by his warnings against standardization, his attraction to free forms, his humanistic vision of the industrial world, especially his work with wood and his many allusions to the shapes of the Finnish Fjords.

Their work on plywood, begun in 1940 with Eero Saarinen – who was also heavily influenced by Aalto – is at the origin of all the Eameses' conquests. It allowed a tremendous amount of research on organics: how could so-called "hard" materials be made compatible with the curves and flexibility of the human body?

The plywood used to make the *Plywood Chair* (numerous versions: high or low, with metal or wooden legs) was first softened, then formed, and finally rigidified in its final shape. Remade by Vitra in 1996, the Plywood Chair remains one of the great musts in the history of contemporary armchairs.

As its name indicates, the *Fiberglass Chair* (1950-1953) is made of fiberglass which is softened by injecting synthetic resin to form a very hard shell.

The most sculptural of the Eames chairs, and the most stunning too, is probably *La Chaise* (1948), named after the *Floating Sculpture* (1927) by Gaston Lachaise. This fiberglass armchair is made from a single mold and rests on a strange metal and wood base: a steel tube frame on an oak crossbar. The chair was not produced during the designers' lifetimes, but has been manufactured by Vitra since 1991.

The *Wire Chair* (1951-1953), made entirely of chrome-plated steel wire, is a tribute to lightness and transparency. Like a Calder mobile, "it puts art at the service of everyday life": its forms, rounded into "a sort of basket supporting the body[8]" contradict the linear, graphic design of the metal mesh.

The *Lounge Chair* – through the expressiveness of its plywood shells, its thick upholstery and its *Ottoman* – symbolizes comfort. The contrast of the materials used – leather, wood and metal – and its supple, sloping lines accentuate the effect. It was not originally intended for mass-production, but it has been produced continuously and often copied. The first model was offered to a great friend of the Eameses, the filmmaker Billy Wilder. Today, this armchair may seem dated, but it has become a classic, representative of a sort of eternal style. We can see that it is not a contemporary product, but it remains a modern interpretation of an English club chair. "I wanted the *Lounge Chair* to have the warm receptive look of a well-used first baseman's mitt[9]," Charles Eames would say.

The idea of structure reaches its apex with the *Aluminum Group*, whose elegant metal frame supports a thin cover of leather or cloth. A gem of industrial design, this elegant series of armchairs embodies both solemnity and a mastered richness of detail. "The details are not details – they make the product. In fact, it is these details that give life to the product[10]," said Charles. The *Aluminum Group* has withstood the test of time (it continues to be a bestseller in highend office furniture), probably because when it was designed in 1958, it was far ahead of its time. With its carved shapes and fine profile, it challenged the strict and sometimes rigid geometry of other models and of modernism, introducing true technological innovations.

Along the same lines, there followed the *Tandem Sitting*, seating for public areas and airports, and the *Soft Pad*, whose seat and back had thicker, softer leather upholstery.

This fascination with materials led the Eameses to take advantage of the new field of "gluing" (as an industrial process), mixing "material qualities and the cultural association of opposites: hard and soft, shiny and dull, technology and everyday life[11]." In addition to the aesthetic and comfort aspects, most of their chairs also featured distinctive elements that were easy to replace, repair or recycle. This concern for the environment so early on makes the designs more contemporary than ever.

From Herman Miller to Vitra

During World War II, Charles and Ray Eames put the molded plywood technology at the service of the US Navy. In 1941-1942, they produced splints to immobilize the legs of wounded soldiers. Thanks to the successful mass-production of these strong, supple and inexpensive splints, they founded the Plyformed Wood Co. in Los Angeles.

In 1943, Edward S. Evans, owner of the Evans Products Co., based in Detroit, purchased the rights to produce and distribute these preformed wooden splints. Plyformed Wood Co. moved its production unit to Venice, California, and was renamed the Molded Plywood Division. Evans Products took over splint production, while Molded Plywood Division experimented with other formed plywood products, such as the chairs and furniture for children that the Eameses had designed in 1945. The goal was to develop a technology that could mass-produce high-quality, curved wood shapes at low cost.

In 1946, when some of their experimental chairs and other plywood furniture were exhibited at the MoMA, they attracted the interest of Dirk Jan De Pree, President of the Herman Miller Furniture Co., and its design director, architect George Nelson. D. J. De Pree was looking for an opportunity to revive his modern furniture company. The Eameses' furniture seemed the perfect fit.

In 1947, Herman Miller acquired the exclusive rights to distribute the furniture. The Venice factory was closed and transferred to Grand Haven, Michigan. In 1949, Herman Miller purchased the rights for the Eames chairs from Evans Products, and the industrial facilities involved in their production were moved to Zeeland, Michigan.

From that point on, the many models made of formed plywood – and later of molded plastic – and the Eameses' taste for and mastery of the technology, allowed them to establish new industrial production standards that remain unequaled.

In 1957, Vitra, a leading Swiss furniture company specializing in high-end office furniture, produced the Eames furniture under license from the American company Herman Miller, and finally acquired the European rights in 1984. Today, Vitra manufactures most of the Eames models for Europe and the Middle East. They are its flagship product line.

Rolf Fehlbaum, its president – a cultivated industrialist who owns the largest European collection of Eames prototypes and original pieces in his museum, the Vitra Design Museum in Germany – has a boundless admiration for Charles Eames: "He was someone who knew how to answer every need, whether it was aesthetic or functional...He had that gift for finding the right formula, and for synthesizing. He was the first to apply new technologies to furniture. A Master[12]..."

A Humanistic Vision

As a bottomless source of inspiration for successive generations of designers, Eames furniture is still appreciated today because it conveys the generous social ideals of its designers.
At once "products and producers of American modernity[13]" (more pragmatic than ideological), this furniture has also satisfied an emotional need that the "cold," more "right-angled" modernism of the Bauhaus tended to ignore. Through their experiments with nature's forms, the two designers made the expression of the technology "gentler." Not that they invented the organic language, but they had the opportunity to combine it with industry, thus creating free forms that allowed multiple spatial arrangements.
Both Charles and Ray also liked little things like toys, primitive objects and "popular" culture, which led them to associate the concept of modernity with "prettiness." While avoiding the "decorative" pitfall, they sought to give a contemporary interpretation to the deep-down and archaic needs of people.
"Design is recognition of a need. Art comes after[14]," Charles would say.
Their passionate, pluridisciplinary and experimental practices revolutionized design and the role of designers. Forty years of work in common fostered an impressive and prolific output. Between 1945 and 1960, developing furniture comprised a large share of the

Eameses' activity, but they also produced more than 25 films, a large number of exhibitions and a multitude of children's toys and games. After 1960, they focused on audiovisual and multimedia projects, and on creating exhibits, in particular for IBM.

Their entire career unfolded in their Venice office, the famous, hectic Eames Office that was at once "museum, playroom, film studio and design workshop[15]."

Charles died on August 21st, 1978. Ray died in 1988, ten years later to the day.

The Eames spirit lives on.

1. FITOUSSI (Brigitte), interview with Rolf Fehlbaum for the catalog *Repères*, Salon du Meuble in Paris, January 1997.
2. PIÑA (Leslie), *Classic Herman Miller*, Schiffer Publishing Ltd., United States, 1998.
3. KIRKHAM (Pat), *Charles and Ray Eames, Designers of the Twentieth Century*, MIT Press, London, 1995.
4. *ditto*.
5. *Eames Vitra*, Weil am Rheim, Vitra, Germany, 1996.
6. KIRKHAM (Pat), *op. cit.*
7. FITOUSSI (Brigitte), *op. cit.*
8. *Eames Vitra, op. cit.*
9. *ditto*.
10. *ditto*.
11. *ditto*.
12. BENAIM (Laurence), "Charles Eames le pionnier des années cinquante," *Marie Claire Maison*, section Créateurs du XXe siècle, n° 285, June 1992.
13. *Eames Vitra, op. cit.*
14. NEUHART (John and Marilyn), *Eames Design, The Work of the Office of Charles and Ray Eames*, Thames & Hudson, London, 1989.
15. *Eames Vitra, op. cit.*

BEWARE
OF IMITATIONS

ENJOY THE COMFORT OF THE
REAL THING
Designed by Charles EAMES for HERMAN MILLER, Inc.

These
are the
ORIGINALS!

Accept
no
substitutes

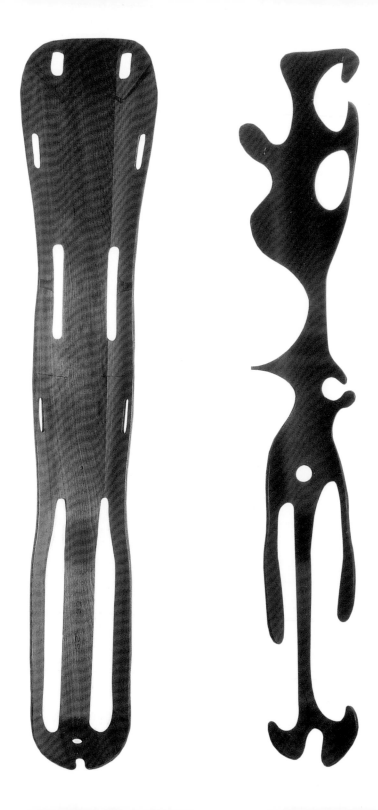

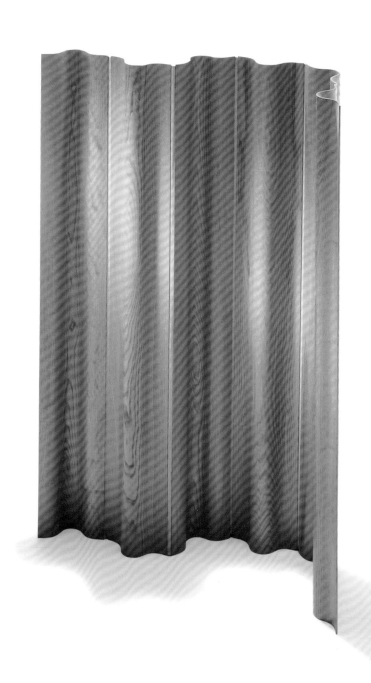

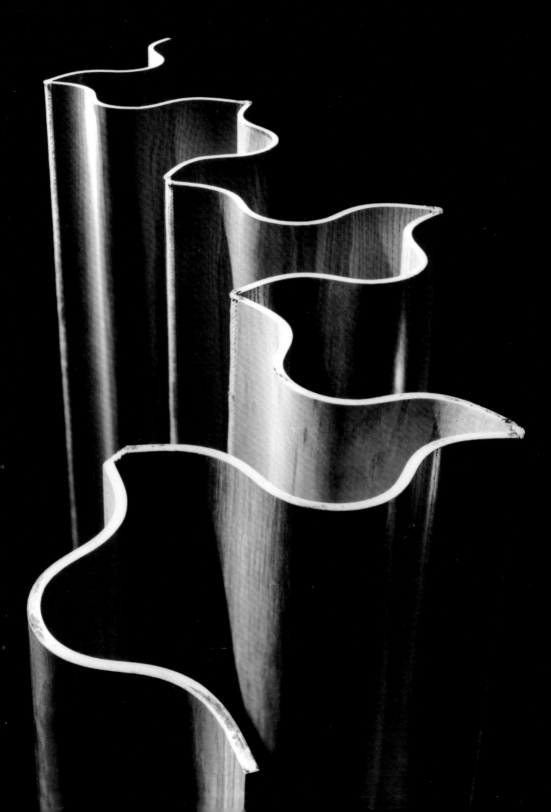

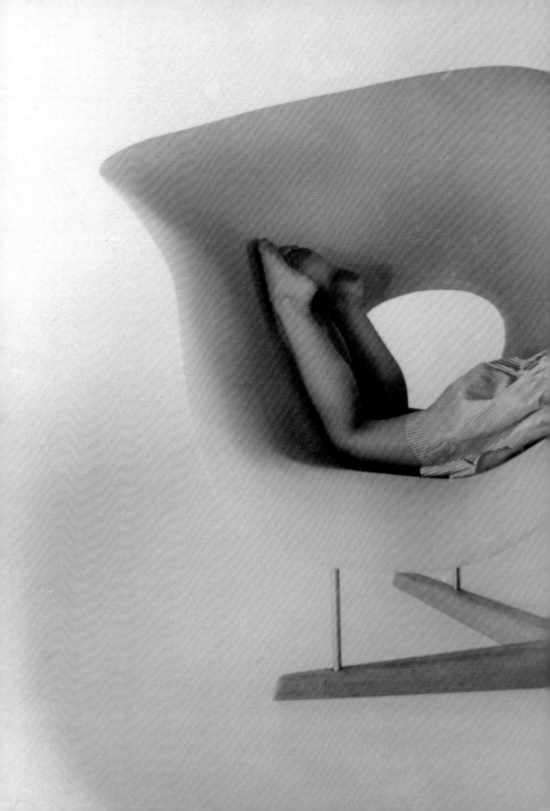

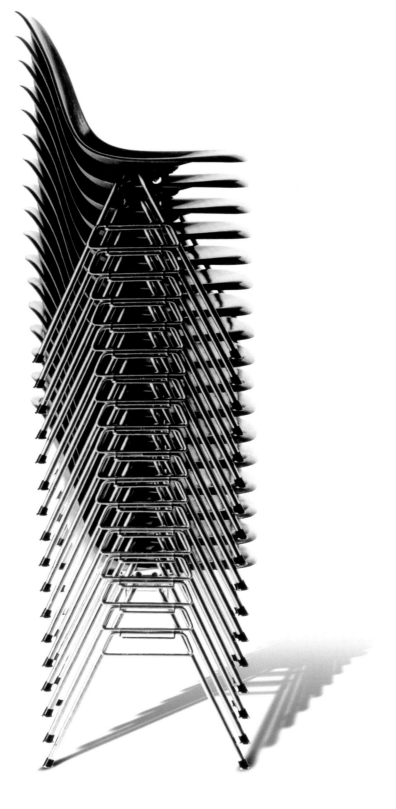

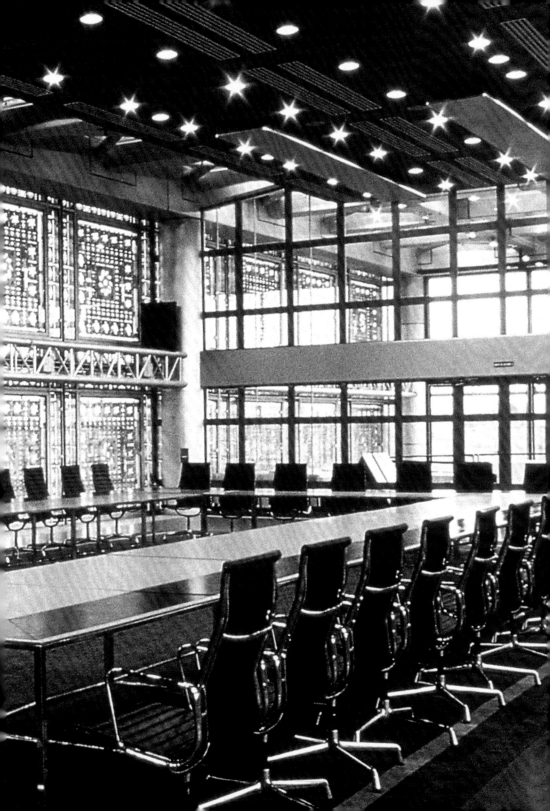

Chronology

1907: Birth of Charles Ormond Eames, Jr., on June 17th in Saint Louis, Missouri.

1912: Birth of Bernice Alexandra Kaiser on December 15th in Sacramento, California. Nicknamed Ray-Ray, then Ray, in 1954 she changed her legal name to Ray Bernice Alexandra Kaiser.

1925: Charles enters Washington University in Saint Louis, majoring in Architecture.

1928: He leaves the university after receiving two honor prizes for the "ultramodernity" of his architectural projects.

1929: He marries Catherine Dewey Woermann, whom he met at Washington University. The couple takes their honeymoon in Europe to discover the great modern architects.

1930: Catherine and Charles return to Saint Louis. On October 11th, a daughter, Lucia Dewey Eames, is born. That year, Charles opens an architectural office with Charles M. Gray, called Gray and Eames.

1931: Ray moves to New York with her mother. Her brother Maurice lives there already.

1933: She begins to study painting with Hans Hofmann who was inaugurating an art school in New York City. She takes classes with him until 1939.

1934: Economic depression: Charles has few architectural orders. He goes to Mexico City for eight months.

1935: Back in Saint Louis, he opens a new office with Robert T. Walsh called Eames and Walsh. They design small houses and churches together. One of his projects, published in the magazine *Architectural Forum*, catches the eye of the Finnish architect Eliel Saarinen.

1937: Ray's paintings are exhibited at the Riverside Museum in New York as part of the first exhibit of the American Abstract Artists, of which she is a member.

1938: Eliel Saarinen, director of the Cranbrook Academy of Art in Bloomfield Hills, Michigan, proposes that Charles come study architecture and design in his school.

1939-1940: Charles becomes head of the Industrial Design Department at Cranbrook, and continues to work part-time at the Saarinen office.

1940: Charles meets Ray at Cranbrook, where she had registered in September. Charles and Eero Saarinen enter the *Organic Design in Home Furnishing* competition organized by the MoMA. They win first prize with molded plywood furniture for which they invented a new manufacturing technique.

1941: Charles and Catherine divorce in May. On June 20th, Charles marries Ray in Chicago, Illinois. In July, they move to California.

1942: They manufacture molded plywood splints for the US Navy using the same technique as for their chairs. In Los Angeles, they found Plyformed Wood and Co.

1943: Evans Products Co. buys the production and distribution rights for the preformed wood splints. Plyformed Wood and Co. is renamed Molded Plywood Division and moves to Venice.

Charles Eames, in his office in Case Study House no. 8, *in Pacific Palisades, California.*
© Photo: Julius Shulman.

1945: The Eameses create molded plywood furniture for children and experiment with this material on a full line of chairs.

1946: Design of the *Plywood Chairs LCW and DCW (Lounge and Dining Chairs with Wood legs)*. In March, they are exhibited with a collection of coffee tables, folding tables and children's furniture at the New York Museum of Modern Art.

1947: Following the MoMA exhibit, Herman Miller Furniture and Co. acquires the exclusive distribution rights for Eames furniture.

1948: Design of *La Chaise*, a fiberglass armchair made from a single mold and manufactured for the first time by Vitra in 1991.

1949: Charles and Ray build their house in Pacific Palisades, near Santa Monica, California. It had been designed in 1947 with Eero Saarinen as part of the *Case Study Houses* program. Herman Miller purchases the rights for the Eames chairs and furniture from Evans Products.

1950-1953: Design of the first molded plastic and fiberglass chairs, *Fiberglass Armchair* and *Fiberglass Chair*, and of the *Elliptical Table Rod Base*.

1951-1953: Design of the *Wire Chair*, entirely in chrome-plated steel wire.

1954: Design of the *Sofa Compact*.

1955: Design of the plastic stackable chair *Fiberglass Stacking Chair*.

1956: Design of the *Lounge Chair* and its *Ottoman* for the birthday of filmmaker Billy Wilder, a close friend of the Eameses.

1957: The Swiss firm Vitra produces Eames furniture, licensed by the American company Herman Miller.

1958: Design of the *Aluminum Group*. Today, it is still one of the best-selling pieces of high-end office furniture.

1960: Design of the *Lobby Chair* and the wood *Stools*.

1961: Design of the *Fonda Chair*.

1962: Design of the airport seat *Tandem Sitting*, a derivative of the *Aluminum Group*.

1964: Design of the institutional *Contract Tables*, a system of tabletops and underframes with multiple form, size and material combinations.

1968: Design of the *Soft Pad*, a lounge chair with leather upholstery.

1969: Design of the *Soft Pad Group* office armchair, a variation of the *Aluminum Group*, with thicker upholstery.

1971: Design of the *Loose Cushion Armchair*, a plastic shell with molded polyurethane upholstery.

1978: Charles Eames dies on August 21st. From then on, Ray directs the Eames Office with its 10-person staff.

1984: Vitra acquires the rights for Eames furniture in Europe and the Middle East. The Eames Office produces its last piece of furniture, the *Teak and Leather Sofa*, a leather sofa with armrests.

1988: Ray Eames dies on August 21st.

Segmented Base Tables, *1964. Institutional tables to be arranged. Variations in height, width and the shape and material of the table-tops are available. The segmented underframe is the basic module.* © Vitra.

Eames

Upholstered version of *Plastic Armchairs* (all forms), *Wire Chair, Plastic Armchair* and *Fonda Chair.* Herman Miller Furniture and Co. © Herman Miller, Inc./photo: West Dempster.
Advertisement warning against Eames imitations for Herman Miller Products, 1963. © Herman Miller, Inc.

Leg splint made of molded plywood, manufactured for the US Navy, 1942-1944 (left). Sculpture in same material by Ray Eames, around 1943 (right). © D.R. **Experimental *Wire Armchair*** made of steel wire, 1951 (prototype). © Vitra Design Museum.

Hang-it-All **coat rack,** designed in 1953 for Tigrett Enterprises. © Herman Miller, Inc./photo: Phil Schaafsma.
Tripod chair made of metal and molded plywood. First version with three legs of *Plywood Chair DCM (Dining Chair with Metal legs),* 1945-1946. Eames Office © 1999 www.eamesoffice.com.

Charles and Ray Eames, in 1958, checking the points whese the fabric fastens onto an *Aluminum Group* armchair being assembled. Eames Office © 1999 www.eamesoffice.com.

Front of Eames house, in Pacific Palisades, California, 1949. The main living area and office are separated by an inner court. Eames Office © 1999 www.eamesoffice.com.

Plywood Chair LCW, (*Lounge Chair with Wood legs*), front and side view, low version, made of molded natural ash plywood, 1946. Remade by Vitra, 1996. © Herman Miller, Inc./photos: Phil Schaafsma.

Folding *Screen* made of natural oak plywood with flexible hinges, 1946. Still produced. © Herman Miller, Inc./photo: Phil Schaafsma (left). © Photo: James Wojcik (right).

Inside view of living room of John Entenza, director of the magazine *Art & Architecture*. This house was built in 1950 by Charles Eames and Eero Saarinen as part of the *Case Study Houses* program. House adjacent to the Eames house in Pacific Palisades, near Santa Monica, California. © Photo: Julius Shulman.

Composition of a series of flagship Eames chairs: *Plywood Chair LCM (Lounge Chair with Metal legs), Plywood Chair DCM (Dining Chair with Metal legs), Plastic Side Chair, Plastic Armchair and Plywood Chair DCM.* © Herman Miller, Inc./photo: Earl Woods.

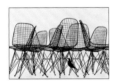

Wire Mesh Chairs **composition with wood bird,** a sculpture belonging to the Eames collection. This photograph by Charles Eames was used to advertise the chair, around 1951. Eames Office © 1999 www.eamesoffice.com.

Charles and Ray Eames at the foot of their office, pinned down by the metal frames of the *Plywood Chair DCM (Dining Chair with Metal legs),* in 1947. The photo was taken by Don Albinson from their roof. Eames Office © 1999 www.eamesoffice.com.

La Chaise lounge chair, 1948. Designed for filmmaker Billy Wider, a friend of the Eameses, it was intended for napping. The chair features six stationary leather cushions and two movable cushions; injected aluminum underframe. © Herman Miller, Inc.

Tandem Sling Seating airport seats, 1962. Photographed at John Wayne Airport in Orange County, California, 1993. © Herman Miller, Inc./Photo: Nick Merrick.

Interior stairway in Eames house, in Pacific Palisades, California, 1949. © Photo: Julius Shulman.
Plastic Armchair, **version with thin metal underframe,** 1950-1953. Opaque plastic shell (fiberglass and resin). Eames Office © 1999 www.eamesoffice.com.

La Chaise **fiberglass armchair,** designed for the *International Competition for Low-Cost Furniture Design,* organized by the New York Museum of Modern Art, in 1948. Never produced during the designers' lifetimes, it has been manufactured by Vitra since 1991. Eames Office © 1999 www.eamesoffice.com.

LCM *(Lounge Chair with Metal legs)* and **CTM** *(Coffee Table with Metal legs)* from the *Plywood* **series,** 1946. Version in molded black ash plywood and chrome-plated steel. Remade by Vitra, 1996. © Vitra.

Stack of children's molded plywood stools and chairs, created in 1945 and produced that same year by the Molded Plywood Division of Evans Products in Venice, California. **Side view of a stack of** *Stacking Chairs,* **or** *Fiberglass Chairs.* With its molded plastic shell, it was the first plastic chair to be manufactured industrially (1955). Vitra stopped producing it in 1993 for environmental reasons. Eames Office © 1999 www.eamesoffice.com (left and right).

Plywood Chair DCM *(Dining Chair with Metal legs),* molded walnut plywood with steel frame. The plywood panel used to make it is first softened, then formed, and then rigidified into its final shape. © Herman Miller, Inc./Photo Earl Woods.
Kitchen at Pacific Palisades house. © Photo: Julius Shulman.

Series of experimental molded plywood chairs, precursors of the *Plywood Chair* series, 1945. Eames Office © 1999 www.eamesoffice.com.
Detailed view of Plywood Chair, 1946. © Photo: James Wojcik.

Charles and Ray Eames in their living room in Pacific Palisades, in the late '50s. © Photo: Julius Shulman.

Metal mold made to mass-produce chairs, for the *International Competition for Low-Cost Furniture Design* organized by the New York Museum of Modern Art, 1948. Eames Office © 1999 www.eamesoffice.com.

Aluminum Group office armchair, 1958. A flagship Eames armchair, still manufactured. Swivel version on five-branch underframe with dual-wheel casters, semi-high back and armrests. Adjustable height by gas cartridge. Chrome-plated injected aluminum frame. © Herman Miller, Inc./Photo: Phil Schaafsma.

Eameses' living room in Pacific Palisades, California, 1949. © Photo: Julius Shulman.

Institut du Monde Arabe, Paris, 1981-1987, built by Jean Nouvel, Gilbert Lézènes, Pierre Soria and Architecture Studio. Salle du Haut Conseil, furnished with *Aluminum Group* armchairs. © D.R.

Back view of *Aluminum Group*, high version without armrests, 1968. The injected aluminum profiles are tensioned near the seat back by clips that stretch the cover. *Fonda Chairs*, chair and small armchair, 1961, designed for the restaurant *La Fonda Del Sol* in New York City, in the *Time & Life* building. The reinforced fiberglass shell was molded in shapes similar to those of the *Plastic Armchair* and the *Side Chair*. Eames Office © 1999 www.eamesoffice.com (left and right).

Modular *Eames Storage Units (ESU)*, 1950. Industrially manufactured furniture made of plastic and plywood, with chrome-plated steel frame. It was produced by Herman Miller until 1955. © Herman Miller, Inc.

The famous *Lounge Chair* and its *Ottoman*, tested by Dick Hoffman, assembly manager at Herman Miller. This shot is taken from the short film *Eames Lounge Chair*, made by Charles in black and white in 1956, the year the armchair was designed. Eames Office © 1999 www.eamesoffice.com.

Outer view of one side of *Case Study House no. 8*, the Eameses' home in Pacific Palisades, California, 1949. © Photo: Julius Shulman.

Bibliography

DREXLER (Arthur), *Charles Eames, Furniture from the Design Collection*, The Museum of Modern Art, New York, 1973.
Eames Vitra, Vitra, Weil am Rhein (Germany), 1996.
FIELL (Charlotte & Peter), *1000 Chairs*, Taschen, Cologne, 1997.
GUIDOT (Raymond), *Histoire du design 1940-1990*, Hazan, Paris, 1994.
KIRKHAM (Pat), *Charles and Ray Eames, Designers of the Twentieth Century*, MIT Press, London, 1995.
NEUHART (John and Marilyn) and EAMES (Ray), *Eames Design, The Work of the Office of Charles and Ray Eames*, Thames & Hudson, London, 1989.
PINA (Leslie), *Classic Herman Miller*, Schiffer Publishing Ltd, United States, 1998.
SHULMAN (Julius), *Julius Shulman, l'architecture et sa photographie*, Taschen, Cologne, 1998.
STEELE (James) and JENKINS (David), *Pierre Koenig*, Phaidon Press Limited, London, 1998.

The author and publisher wish to thank the Eames Office, Herman Miller, Inc., Vitra and the Vitra Design Museum, and more particularly Eames Demetrios, Shelley Mills, Andreas Nutz, Robert Viol, Rolf Fehlbaum and Bernadette Guntzburger for their help in preparing this book.
Also, thanks to West Dempster, Nick Merrick, Phil Schaafsma, Julius Shulman, James Wojcik and Earl Woods.

EAMES OFFICE
For more information on the work of Charles and Ray Eames: Eames Offices, P. O. Box 268, Venice, California 90294, USA (archives and gallery); Web site: www.eames office.com.
The Eames Office is dedicated to preserving, communicating and extending the work of Charles and Ray Eames: three dimensions that are essential to keeping the office useful and vital. All of Charles's and Ray's work is the result of a way of looking at the world—a design philosophy and process that is worth sharing in many different dimensions. In addition to distributing classic works, the Eames Office launches wholly new works that are consistent with that philosophy.